Cracking the Code

Written by Claire Owen

Ireland

My name is Maeve.
Like the Irish mathematician
Sarah Flannery, I have grown
up in County Cork. Have you
ever used a secret code to
send messages to a friend?
Have you ever been able
to crack a code?

Contents

Wherever you see me, you'll find activities to try and questions to answer.

Irish Mathematicians

Over the years, there have been quite a few famous mathematicians from Ireland. Most of them were men who carried out their most important work as adults. In 1999, however, a 16-year-old Irish girl named Sarah Flannery was hailed as a mathematical genius when she invented a new and much faster code for sending confidential information over the Internet.

In 1999, Sarah's work won her the titles of Irish Young Scientist of the Year and European Young Scientist of the Year. Sarah later wrote a book about her mathematical experiences.

confidential   private; intended to be kept secret

Irish Mathematicians

The Kelvin temperature scale is named after Lord Kelvin, an Irish mathematician and physicist. Lord Kelvin also played an important part in the development of the first telephone cable from Ireland to America.

George Boole was a self-taught English mathematician who became a professor at University College, Cork. He invented Boolean algebra, a binary system of logic that is fundamental to the way computers work.

In 1843, William Rowan Hamilton was walking beside a canal in Dublin when he had a sudden inspiration for a new kind of algebra. He scratched a mathematical formula on the stone wall of a nearby bridge!

binary system a system in which each number is shown by using only the digits 0 and 1

Sarah's System

Sarah Flannery became interested in codes after attending a lecture given by her father, a mathematics teacher. She arranged to spend a week working for a company that creates new codes. There, Sarah pursued an idea that Dr. Michael Purser had begun to investigate but had put aside. Over the months that followed, Sarah developed a coding system that involved prime numbers and matrices.

Prime Numbers

A prime number has only two factors—itself and one. There is no simple pattern or rule for finding prime numbers.

2, 3, 5, 7, 11, 13, 17, 19, 23, 29, 31, 37, 41, 43, 47, 53, 59, 61, 67, 71, 73, 79, 83, 89, 97, 101, 103, 107, 109, 113, 127, 131, 137, 139, 149, 151 ...

Matrices

A matrix is an arrangement of numbers in rows and columns. Sarah's system involved multiplication of 2 x 2 matrices.

$$\begin{bmatrix} 3 & 9 \\ 6 & 8 \end{bmatrix}$$

2 x 2 matrix

$$\begin{bmatrix} 4 & 4 & 1 & 2 \\ 6 & 0 & 7 & 8 \\ 0 & 5 & 3 & 6 \end{bmatrix}$$

3 x 4 matrix

factor   a whole number that divides another whole number without a remainder

6

To Multiply 2 x 2 Matrices

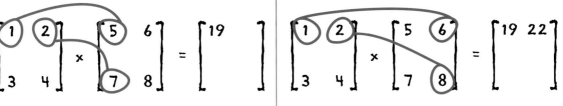

$$\begin{bmatrix} 1 & 2 \\ 3 & 4 \end{bmatrix} \times \begin{bmatrix} 5 & 6 \\ 7 & 8 \end{bmatrix} = \begin{bmatrix} ? & ? \\ ? & ? \end{bmatrix}$$

Step 1: 1st row x 1st column

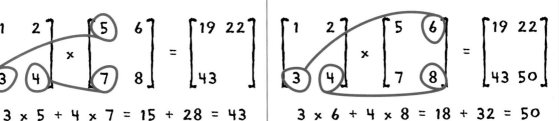

$1 \times 5 + 2 \times 7 = 5 + 14 = 19$

Step 2: 1st row x 2nd column

$1 \times 6 + 2 \times 8 = 6 + 16 = 22$

Step 3: 2nd row x 1st column

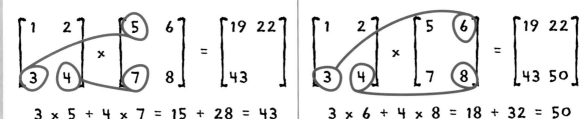

$3 \times 5 + 4 \times 7 = 15 + 28 = 43$

Step 4: 2nd row x 2nd column

$3 \times 6 + 4 \times 8 = 18 + 32 = 50$

Unfortunately, Sarah's system had a flaw in it. When Dr. Purser studied the system closely, he found a way to figure out its hidden prime numbers. Sarah explained this in her book.

Use the steps above to multiply the following matrices.

$$\begin{bmatrix} 1 & 2 \\ 3 & 4 \end{bmatrix} \times \begin{bmatrix} 3 & 5 \\ 2 & 4 \end{bmatrix}$$

7

Hidden Messages

Long before Sarah Flannery developed her coding system, people were investigating methods of sending secret information. These methods can be divided into two categories—hiding the message (steganography) or making the information unintelligible (cryptography). The earliest recorded examples of hidden messages come from the Greek historian Herodotus and are nearly 2,500 years old.

According to Herodotus, a Greek ruler once tattooed a message on the shaved head of a slave. After the hair had grown back, the slave was sent to the ruler's son-in-law, with instructions to shave his head!

unintelligible   not able to be understood

The ancient Greeks wrote with a pointed stick on a wax tablet. Herodotus says that secret messages were sometimes scratched onto the wooden base of the tablet and then covered with wax.

"Cryptography is the science of putting disguises on and of taking them off."
—Sarah Flannery

Did You Know?

Between the 1940s and 1960s, spies used microdot cameras to take photos that could be reduced to a tiny dot. The pinhead-sized photo was then glued onto a period in a piece of writing! In this way, secret information could be hidden in an innocent-looking letter.

9

Caesar's Cipher

Julius Caesar, the commander of the Roman army, is the first person known to have used coded messages. More than 2,000 years ago, Caesar sent messages to his generals in which each letter was replaced by the letter of the alphabet three spaces ahead.

A	B	C	D	E	F	G	H	I	J	K	L	M	N	O	P	Q	R	S	T	U	V	W	X	Y	Z
D	E	F	G	H	I	J	K	L	M	N	O	P	Q	R	S	T	U	V	W	X	Y	Z	A	B	C

The word HURRY, for example, would become KXUUB. This is a very simple kind of code and can be cracked very easily.

crack   (or break) to figure out a code or cipher without having the key

PHHW PH DW
WKH FRUQHU
RI EHHFK
VWUHHW DQG
HOP DYHQXH

The message above was created using Caesar's Cipher. Can you decipher it? Can you figure out the key that was used to create the message below?

Definitions

Code:

A system for replacing each word or phrase with another word, number, or symbol.

- To protect a message in this way is called *encoding*.

Cipher:

A system for replacing each letter with another letter or symbol.

- To protect a message in this way is called *enciphering*.

- A key shows how each letter is enciphered.

Encrypt:

A term that covers both encoding and enciphering.

FBDI MFUUFS
IBT CFFO
SFQMBDFE CZ
UIF OFYU
MFUUFS PG UIF
BMQIBCFU

Did You Know?

Technically, many "codes" are actually ciphers. However, in everyday language, the word *code* is used for both codes and ciphers.

The Pigpen Cipher

It is easy to invent a cipher by creating a symbol for each letter of the alphabet. However, it can be difficult for people to remember 26 new symbols and which letters they represent. An 18th-century code called the Pigpen Cipher avoided this problem by using grids that made the symbols easy to remember. The Pigpen Cipher was used by the Confederate States in the Civil War.

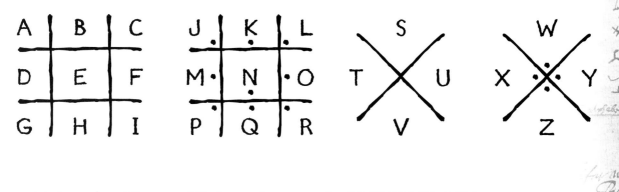

Using the Pigpen Cipher, the words SECRET PLOT become:

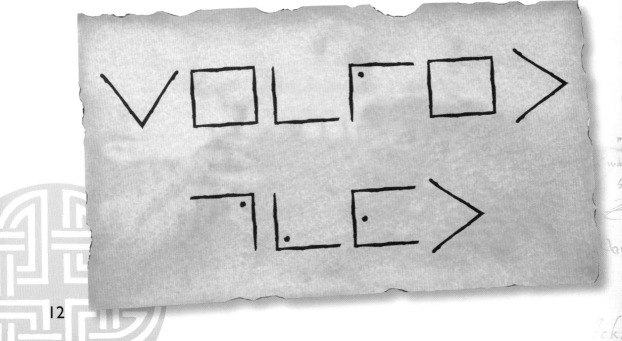

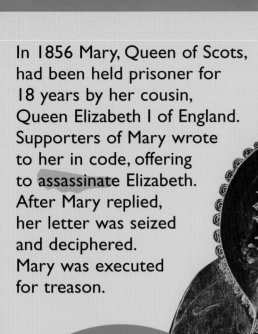

In 1856 Mary, Queen of Scots, had been held prisoner for 18 years by her cousin, Queen Elizabeth I of England. Supporters of Mary wrote to her in code, offering to assassinate Elizabeth. After Mary replied, her letter was seized and deciphered. Mary was executed for treason.

Make up a message and use the Pigpen Cipher to encrypt it. Exchange work with a partner and decipher the message you receive.

The code used by Mary and her supporters was a simple cipher. They substituted each letter of the alphabet with another letter or symbol.

assassinate to murder a political leader

13

Key Words

Another method of creating a cipher involves using a key word or phrase. The key word becomes the first part of the ciphertext, followed by any remaining letters of the alphabet. Here, for example, is the key formed by using the key word ZEBRA:

A key phrase could be the first line of a poem, story, or saying. Any repeated letters are simply dropped. For example, the key formed by using the proverb "Look before you leap" is:

One difficulty in using a cipher like this is that the sender must find a safe way to let the receiver know the key word or phrase.

ciphertext   the letters or symbols that represent A, B, C, and so on

Hmm, so the key word is the 8th word of the 12th line on page 5.

HAPPY
BIRTHDAY
LOVE FROM
LUCY
8/12/05

Figure It Out

1. Use the ZEBRA key to encipher this message.

   LOOK UNDER THE THIRD STONE IN THE PATHWAY.

2. Use the ZEBRA key to decipher this message. (Find each letter in the second row. Write the corresponding letter from the first row.)

   STPL JACS ZS SFA SPZCCGB JGDFSQ ZLR VZGS ZS SFA LAWS KZGJEMW.

3. Create a new cipher using a key word or phrase of your choice. (Make sure that you don't repeat any letters.)

   a. Write a secret message and use your cipher to encrypt it.

   b. Exchange your message with a partner and decipher the message you receive. (Don't forget to exchange key words!)

Over the years, people have found many imaginative ways to pass on a key word. For example, a date might be a clue to the location of the key word.

Looking at Letters

Many ciphers are created by substituting each letter of the alphabet with another letter. Altogether, there are more than 20,000,000,000,000,000,000,000,000,000 different ways this can be done! To break such a code, it would be impossible to check every single key. Instead, code breakers analyze the frequency of the letters used.

Frequency of Letters in English Text (%)

E	12.7	S	6.3	C	2.8	B	1.5
T	9.1	H	6.1	M	2.4	V	1.0
A	8.2	R	6.0	W	2.4	K	0.8
O	7.5	D	4.3	F	2.2	J	0.2
I	7.0	L	4.0	G	2.0	X	0.2
N	6.7	U	2.8	Y	2.0	Z	0.1
				P	1.9	Q	0.1

Count the letters in the text at the right. What percent of those letters are *E*s?

The frequency of the letter *E* in written English is 12.7 percent. This means that, out of every 100 letters, there are (on average) 12 or 13 *E*s.

In the story *The Adventure of the Dancing Men*, the famous fictional detective Sherlock Holmes explains the steps he used to break a cipher that involved picture symbols.

Can you decipher the message above? You will need to figure out three new symbols. (All the others have been used in the column at the right.)

Dancing with Codes

1. Holmes noticed that this symbol occurred most often.

   He guessed that it represented the letter *E*.

2. Holmes substituted *E* for 👤 in:

   He decided that the word must be *LEVER*, *NEVER*, or *SEVER*, and *NEVER* made the most sense.

3. After Holmes substituted the letters *N*, *V*, and *R* for the appropriate pictures, he was able to guess other words.

4. Continuing in this way, Holmes was able to create this message to trick the villain of the story:

C O M E   H E R E

A T   O N C E

Counting Letters

The frequency of letters in a short piece of text can be significantly different from the average frequencies shown on page 16. In general, the longer a piece of text, the closer the letter frequencies will be to the long-term averages. For this reason, analyzing letter frequencies is not always a suitable method for deciphering short messages.

Hmm, I wonder which symbol stands for E?

PARKING FINE

Look at this paragraph. Why is it unusual? Don't just zip through it quickly but study it scrupulously. Can you spot what is unusual about it? If not, look again. Try not to miss a word or symbol. It truly isn't all that difficult!

scrupulous   thorough; paying attention to details

Graphing Letter Frequencies

You will need paper, a newspaper article (an enlarged copy if possible), a copy of the Blackline Master, and a colored marker or pencil.

1. List the letters A through Z on a sheet of paper. Count 200 letters in your newspaper article.

> The technology of secret communication is called cryptology. It has two parts: communications security, known as COMSEC, and communications intelligence, known as COMINT. People use communications security to make and keep messages secret.

2. Cross out one word at a time, making a tally mark for each letter in that word. Then add the tallies for each letter. (Check that your total is 200.)

A	⊥⊥⊥⊥ ⊥⊥⊥⊥ ///
B	—
C	⊥⊥⊥⊥ ⊥⊥⊥⊥ ⊥⊥⊥⊥ ////
D	///
E	⊥⊥⊥⊥ ⊥⊥⊥⊥ ⊥⊥⊥⊥ ⊥⊥⊥⊥ /
F	\
G	////\
H	////
I	⊥⊥⊥⊥ ⊥⊥⊥⊥ ⊥⊥⊥⊥
J	—
K	////
L	⊥⊥⊥⊥ //
M	⊥⊥⊥⊥ ⊥⊥⊥⊥
N	⊥⊥⊥⊥ ⊥⊥⊥⊥ ⊥⊥⊥⊥ ///

> The technology of secret commun is called cryptology. It has two par communications security, known a: COMSEC, and communications intelligence, known as COMINT. People use communications security to make and keep messages secret.

3. Work with 4 other students so that you have 1,000 letters in all. For each letter A through Z, find the frequency in 1,000 letters. Then divide by 10 to find the percent.

	Me	Tim	Sam	Jamal	Josh	Frequency (in 1,000)	%
A	13	17	15	24	19	88	8.8
B	0	2	8	3	3	16	1.6
C	19	3	0	4	6	32	3.2
D	3	10	11	6	10	40	4.0

4. Color bars on the graph to show the percents.

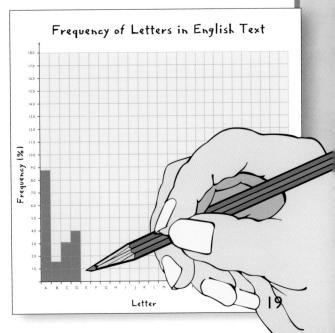

Frequency of Letters in English Text

19

Dot, Dot, Dot

Not all codes were designed to keep messages secret.
Morse Code, for example, was invented for a very different
reason. The earliest telegraph system, invented in Germany
in 1809, had 26 wires, one for each letter of the alphabet.
This system proved to be impractical, however. In 1838,
American Samuel Morse invented a code of dots and dashes
that could be sent along one wire using short and long
pulses of electric current.

Morse Code

A	•—	B	—•••
C	—•—•	D	—••
E	•	F	••—•
G	——•	H	••••
I	••	J	•———
K	—•—	L	•—••
M	——	N	—•
O	———	P	•——•
Q	——•—	R	•—•
S	•••	T	—
U	••—	V	•••—
W	•——	X	—••—
Y	—•——	Z	——••

Morse assigned the simplest codes to
E and *T*, the letters that are used most
frequently.

telegraph   a system for sending messages using a code of electrical
             signals sent through a wire or by radio

Braille is a code of raised dots that enables blind people to read and write. It was invented in 1829 by Louis Braille, a 20-year-old Frenchman who had been blind since the age of three.

Braille

A   B   C   D   E   F   G   H   I   J

K   L   M   N   O   P   Q   R   S   T

U   V   W   X   Y   Z

Decide with a partner how you could make short sounds for dots and longer sounds for dashes. Then practice "sending" your name in Morse Code.

Did You Know?

Some Morse Code operators could send or "read" up to 60 words per minute!

Cryptography Today

The development of machines and computers has made it possible to create ciphers that are more and more complex. However, at the same time, technology has made it possible to break such ciphers! Modern cryptographers agree that there is no such thing as an unbreakable cipher. They focus on protecting the keys that they use, rather than on trying to keep their encryption methods secret.

The most famous cipher machine is the Enigma. This German invention was used to encrypt messages during World War II. It took many years of work by Polish and British mathematicians to break the Enigma cipher.

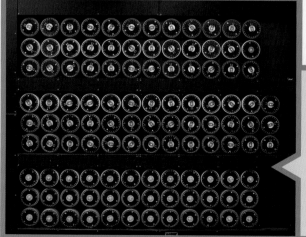

The Bombe decryption machine was used in England to decrypt, or crack, messages made with the Enigma.

Today, huge amounts of information are sent electronically all around the world. More than ever before, governments, organizations, and individuals need to keep information secure.

Sample Answers

Page 7

$$\begin{bmatrix} 1 & 2 \\ 3 & 4 \end{bmatrix} \times \begin{bmatrix} 3 & 5 \\ 2 & 4 \end{bmatrix} = \begin{bmatrix} 7 & 13 \\ 17 & 31 \end{bmatrix}$$

Page 11
MEET ME AT THE CORNER OF BEECH STREET AND ELM AVENUE

Each letter has been replaced by the next letter of the alphabet.

Page 15
1. JMMI TLRAP SFA SFGPR QSMLA GL SFA NZSFVZX

2. TURN LEFT AT THE TRAFFIC LIGHTS AND WAIT AT THE NEXT MAILBOX

Page 16
22 percent (22 *Es* out of 100 letters)

Page 17
I AM VERY CLEVER

Page 18
The paragraph has no *Es*.

Explore some other codes. For example, you could use numbers to represent letters, or you could reverse the order of the letters in each word (for example, THE END becomes EHT DNE).

Index